A Walking Live Miracle

No More Crying

Rayford Campbell Jr.

Dedication

This book is dedicated to my wife, Shelia Carradine Campbell. She is truly, for me, a direct gift from My God above and everywhere. From the moment we met, when she saw me from afar, I ended up walking toward her. It was no coincidence because it was meant to be.

I thank God for the type of mother she has been and is to this day. She has been so supportive. I could not have a more dedicated wife and partner to experience this life's journey and make it worthwhile. Those who pick up this book know that the spirit is leading you. The spirit breathes life into these pages for you. To my mother, who always reminded me that words have the power to educate and change people's lives. To my grandmother, who gave me the gift of knowing the spirit of dreams and how to fulfill them.

To Rayford Howard Campbell the Third, who has shown patience and dedication to achieving all life offers.

To Tori Deanna Campbell Blackmon, who has shown that smooth determination will work in one's life. To Rashaan Nijel Campbell, who has shown the gift of imagination and is not afraid to implement his ideas, To Morgan Brianna Campbell, who is blessed with a great personality and confidence to go after and pursue things that only God can give a person that kind of determination to go after.

To all of you, I thank you and love you.

Acknowledgment

I am so grateful to the following individuals:

My great-grandmother, Mrs. Georgia McCoy Martin for the love she showed me without ever saying it. My grandmother, Mrs. Mamie Pearl Jackson, for loving me and making me feel very special when I was a child.

To my mother, Mrs. Frankie Lee Lewis Campbell, for never giving up on telling me over and over again to write a book, and finally, our children Rayford Howard Campbell 3rd, Tori Deanna Campbell, Rashad Nijel Campbell, and Morgan Brianna Campbell, for letting me know that children are truly a gift from My God.

My wife, Shelia Carradine Campbell, is the true love of my life. The love that only My God could have sent into my life, and the one that has always been there with me truly through the ups, downs, good times, and bad.

Most importantly, I Thank MY GOD for all my life's spiritual, physical, emotional, and friendly blessings.

About the Author

I'm Rayford Howard Campbell Jr. Recently, I wrote a book called **'A Walking Live Miracle.'** It's a memoir that I think would appeal to all sectors of life. I've lived and experienced several events in my life that the holy spirit has placed upon me to share with you.

I played professional Basketball in Mexico. I graduated from the University of Mobile in Mobile, Alabama. I majored in Organizational Management from the School of Leadership, where I made the National Dean's List. Only one-half of one percent of the Nation's collegiate students make up this list.

I'm a licensed home builder in the states of Alabama and Louisiana. I'm also a real estate investor and have a nonprofit organization called Gulf Coast Community Support Network Inc., which I am now an author. I'm very spiritual and love to share it with everyone I can.

May God bless me with Protecting Hands.

Amen.

Preface

I've lived and experienced several events in my life that the holy spirit has placed upon me to share with you. A few of the main things the reader should take away from this read is the spirit of never giving up. Learn from all experiences, and be confident in calling on the Most High, along with My God's blessings and reading this informative book. It will save you from much pain and disappointment and help you grow spiritually beyond your belief.

Contents

Chapter 1: Early Childhood

Families are a blessing; they always have been.

I will start with my great-grandmother, who was a white lady. I was the eldest great-grandson to her. She lived in the deep south and had moved from Natchez, Mississippi. She had a brother who moved to Chicago and became a self-made millionaire, and he tried to bring my great-grandmother and her sister there.

She didn't like the plan, so she and her sister moved to Grove Hill, Alabama. So, they moved to Mobile, Alabama, when she got on her feet. The second largest city in Alabama. Now there, she brought her five daughters, one of whom was my grandmother.

Now, my grandmother had one daughter, and she was my mother.

My grandmother got pregnant by Johnnie Lewis (my grandfather), the great-great-grandson of Cudjoe Lewis from the Clotilda story. Clotilda's story was a famous historical event. It was the last known illegal slave ship to arrive in the U.S. The slave ship (Clotilda) had brought kidnapped Africans to Mobile, Alabama, because of a bet between two white men, Timothy Meaher and another guy, which was illegal.

The African captives were transferred to river barges, and then the captain burned the Clotilda to hide the evidence of the voyage. Perhaps Cudjoe Lewis was the third to last adult survivor of the Atlantic slave trade between Africa and the United States. Cudjoe Lewis was mentioned in several books, and many journalists and authors are still writing about him. My aunt, my mother's younger half-sister, gave all this information to a lady writing another book. This incident on the captive African migrants had already gained popularity through multiple articles and books.

A Quick Departure And Return:

The husband and the wife should get out of bed (if possible) at the same time each day. Stand and pray to the Lord a short prayer of thanks for giving you both another day, a day you've never seen before and will never see again. That means that yesterday is gone, and you will never see it again. You will likely see another Monday, Tuesday, Wednesday, Thursday, Friday, Saturday, and Sunday. However, you will never know the time and space of the previous day again. So, when we say yesterday is history, tomorrow is a mystery because you do not know what it holds or if MY GOD will let you see it. Today is a gift. That is why it is called the PRESENT. So, we must not forget or take for granted that MY GOD has given us another NEW day. You will also find that I will refer to God as MY GOD. Know he is all of our gods. However, when I sometimes refer to God as MY GOD. I should be possessive of him because I love him and know what he means to me.

However, returning to my grandmother, she was half white and half Indian. Her only daughter was my mother, who had me when she was just 16. My grandmother raised me, my sister, and my brother all of our lives, and we were very close to her. I had seen my mother and knew she was very strong. My mother married an Indian man from Monessen, Pennsylvania. His name was Rayford Campbell Senior. He migrated to Mobile, Alabama, with his one brother and two sisters and lived with their relatives. They were not very rich but were well off. My father was raised with his relatives. So apparently, after a few years, my father and mother met and fell in love.

My father impregnated my mother at 16, and they had me—Rayford Campbell Junior. One of my father's jobs was a wholesaler of Moonshine, an illegal liquor. He had several guys take the Moonshine and deliver it to houses, and I remember making a delivery once at night to an old lady. I was only seven years old. They got married and then had a daughter and another son. I have two younger siblings, Trenia Yoland Campbell and Frankie Cardinas Campbell. My parents showed care, love, and attraction toward one another. They were happy together until my father's girlfriends emerged from the woodwork. My mother did not put up well with this situation.

There hasn't been a single woman on this planet who would like to live with a cheating husband. The new lust of my father ruined their happy marriage; there were endless fights and arguments between them. Ultimately, it led to a broken marriage. Later, they divorced; I was eight when they separated.

A Quick Departure And Return:

You should know that you are a miracle for other people. This is why you must face the enemy, other negative things, and forces in life. You will have chosen to be one of the many things that MY GOD has for you on your journey with MY GOD. Now, back to the story. My father was very handsome, lively, and fun to be around. After my parents' divorce, my father went to

Washington, DC, where his relatives migrated and later remarried. Maybe he was planning on having more sons, but God gifted him six beautiful daughters instead and a lovely wife, too.

I must say his daughters are beautiful, all of them. And I, as their half-brother, had a good understanding with my half-sisters, especially the oldest and second oldest daughters, as they were closer to me in age.

My mother graduated and went into nursing but did not practice it rigorously. However, she had friends who were professional doctors and nurses who were still in practice. My mother was a beautiful individual. The professional circle of people around her loved her. My father had already remarried and lived a good life.

A Quick Departure And Return:

Society has different houses for us all: the crazy house, the jail house, and the grave house. Then, the survivors left here on this earth have two options regarding home choices. The house of God or the house of Satan. The first thought that comes to mind regarding the house of God is the church, which is the house that I'm referring to. However, let us approach this from a spiritual and mental point of view. When we are on this earth, we make choices every day. The options are simple: either good or bad, Godly or evil. Honestly, there are different levels of these decisions. The ones you make will take you to your father, either MY GOD or Satin.

Now, we can peel the onion back even more. Once Jesus was teaching in the temple, he ended the class, and one of the good-hearted people said to Jesus, *"Master, we don't understand."* Jesus knew that He was telling the truth because He is MY GOD, and He knows everything. So, Jesus went back over the lesson in a way everyone understood. However, after the lesson, one in the class came to Jesus and said that he and maybe a few more individuals did not understand. Jesus did not ask him what he did not understand. He is God, and He knew that the person was lying. Jesus said that you are of your father, the Devil. He is a liar and a murderer and stays true to his character. So, with that example, which choice will you make in this life? Be a true warrior and believer for MY GOD and Father, or a liar and trickery person for the one which will be your father, in this case, the Devil. Now, back to the story.

So later, my mother also had a second marriage to a man who was never in her league. He was a great man; he made my mother happy, but they had two different career choices.

My step-father had an air-conditioning business; he was a professional repairman, and that was his skillset. But he earned a good living and provided a comfortable lifestyle for my mother. Soon after some time, my mother and my stepfather started having arguments, which led my mother to drink. Even when she was drunk, she acted fine.

My grandmother raised my siblings and me. She was very generous and loved us with all of her heart. Our grandmother was a blessing. She was very generous to us and, most importantly, listened to our wants and fulfilled them. She pretty much spoiled us. Considering our appearance, we were all very good-looking. We went to a private school and focused on our studies. My grandmother was very possessive about us. She would buy us everything that we asked for. We were not rich back in our childhood, but we believed we were well off in our poor little neighborhood.

I owned a minibike and had almost everything I wanted as a child. I was blessed in numerous ways. I was the eldest and the most caring brother to my siblings. My sister was a year younger than me, but we were not very close. We didn't have a strong bond because I always looked at her as a child. The best thing is we never argued or had useless fights in the house. It was very peaceful in the house, but as time passed, my sister and I became close and started bonding.

Then, I had a younger brother four years younger than me and three years younger than our sister. Little children in the house get pampered the most, so my grandmother always took extra care of him, and he would never stop with his innocent little demands. We three siblings had a bond based more on respect than anything else. There wasn't any instance when my younger siblings misbehaved with me or retaliated to my demands. I was always taken as an elder brother and given due respect.

A Quick Getaway And Return:

Our bodies are one of the most perfect things on this earth, and I feel God has made them. I want you to concentrate carefully on what I'm about to say. It's good for any coach of a team or leader of a group. Please imagine one's entire body as one powerful entity with all its functional parts and their importance. Now, think of a group or a team. Each person is as important as each part of the human body. One person might possess the gift of being cerebral, while another might have the never-give-up spirit, another might have the gift of motivation, and so on. Now, we should make everyone understand that they should put all their talents together like a single balled fist that is one. After that, they must be convinced and believe they should LOVE EACH OTHER AS ONE AND LOVE MY GOD. Then, they will have a super force in whatever field they are in.

Continuing with the story. When I was four, my grandmother left me with her mother's sister to watch over me. Her grandson was there visiting. I don't remember how he did it. However, we ended up in the basement. This is as early as I remember MY GOD saving me. I was about to be molested, and all of a sudden, the cousin heard his grandfather drive up in his car. So, he immediately told me to pull up my pants. My God saved me from something that would have shaped me for the rest of my life.

Chapter 2: Education

My school life was always fun and will remain in my memories forever. We weren't rich, but still, I went to a small Catholic school in a Black neighborhood. I always made friends with older guys and was more interested in what older people invested their time into.

So, after school, I would be with older guys. I started the first grade when I was only four years of age, and I made friends with guys who were six years of age, and they acted like they were looking out for me.

A Quick Departure And Return:

One set of believers has experienced something that has shaken them to their core and changed their way of thinking and their lives. There are other ways of reaching the level I'm speaking of. However, we are going in MY GOD'S direction and the direction of believers who have not experienced the previously mentioned. Do know that MY GOD controls it all, and if He decides to let us experience it or not, it's His choice. Just know that you must believe to your core that He is your everything, and His love is the only thing keeping you and guiding you on this earth.

Then you have the straight-up unbelievers. These are individuals that haven't reached the level of the believers. Either MY GOD hasn't chosen to make it happen for them, or they are fighting the change. Back to the story, the older guys doodled all types of things on the sidewalk. At that time, I never knew their meaning. I couldn't even spell the things that they wrote. But I wanted to fit in with them, so I tried participating in the activity. I only knew the spelling of my name then, so I went to the sidewalk and wrote my name in bold letters. The boys smirked at me, and I never knew why they smiled suspiciously at me.

The next day at school, the teachers and the priest came to me. They were looking at me as if I was someone at fault. I wasn't sure what I'd done wrong.

I didn't know that making a small doodle on the walkway was a criminal offense —vandalism, as they called it.

I got beaten up for it. The Catholic school's management called my mother; she was at her job. My mother worked at a bag mill and had to leave it midway to see what I had been up to.

Other stuff written on the wall was also blamed, but I didn't do it. I told the management about it, but they wouldn't listen. So, I was blamed and beaten.

Another instance was when I was beaten at the Catholic school for misspelling the word Black, and a teacher started beating and scolding me. She wouldn't stop until I spelled it correctly.

I went to Catholic school till the fifth grade; many other students were switching schools, and I had that option, too. I was placed into the proper grade along the way. I left Catholic School for middle school and went to a public school. It was a Black school and very massive. I was old enough to attend the same school that my parents attended. So, I attended Mobile County Training School. Back then, it was known as The Community of Plateau. Now, it is known as Africatown, USA. Many professional baseball players attended the school. It was a high school from sixth to twelfth grade.

I was there at Mobile Training County School in the sixth, seventh, and eighth grades and then returned to the Catholic High School for higher education. I became a legend there and played basketball; I was the main guy in eighth grade and was a basketball player, where I averaged 29.4 points per game, and that was when the game was slower than it is now. I had so many good experiences there. My classmates went to different schools and stayed together, but I went away from them. Later, I returned to a Catholic High School, where I knew only a few people. I became well-known, and people started to get to know me.

A Quick Departure And Return:

The words you say or choose carry much weight; remember, children do not forget. Please don't constantly say negative things to the children, which can shape their lives and guide them in either a good or bad direction. You do not give the same gift to a believer as you do to an unbeliever. Become a great listener. Put the fires out and become a person that promotes peace. Peace is one of the great things emphasized in the Bible's beatitudes. Come to me, Lord, so that I can come to you. And thank you, Lord, for loving me so much that I can love myself, enabling me to love others. Now, back to the story. There was another incident where a guidance counselor accused me of cheating on the A-C-T. I was brilliant but never applied myself to my studies very hard. I was an average student who used to score Cs and a couple of Bs. But basketball saved my life. I also took the

ACT and scored surprisingly well. My result was so unexpected that the guidance counselor asked me. "Who took that test for you?" he asked me. "You cheated, right?"

"I didn't cheat," I told him.

It was true; I didn't cheat. That guy threatened to report me for cheating, but I was not scared. My grades weren't that great, but I was smart.

My grandmother used to bring me big hamburgers for lunch during my elementary school days, and the rest of my classmates had sandwiches and things like that. My grandmother pretty much spoiled me; she would do everything to make me happy, and I loved her a lot. My jealous adult relatives nicknamed me Baby Jesus because my grandmother would not let them discipline me. There were so many memories I made in school. I never had many friends; I was more of a loner, but over time, I became popular because of playing basketball and my athletic aura.

A Quick Getaway And Return.

Make sure that your heart is innocent to be hurt so that you can feel love. There is a spiritual balance there. You must pull in the reigns at times. Also, there are times when you should let the reigns out more. There is a certain amount of risk involved in both of them. These are times that we should be in tune with the Holy Spirit. It should be a way of life. Not waiting to get in these circumstances. Now, let's return to the story.

Chapter 3: The Life-Changing Decision

My favorite leisure activity has always been playing basketball. I was devoted to the game because I had been practicing and playing it since early childhood. A basketball court gave me the most comfortable feeling in the world. That one place boosted my confidence because I loved how great I was there.

My basketball skills developed with time. I was always an average student at school, but due to my extra-curricular activities, mainly basketball, I managed to represent my school. When I played basketball, I felt great. Even though I believed I was the best player, I had injuries too, but the best thing is I maintained a healthy, athletic body.

My obsession with basketball was strange for some people to figure out because it was a different sport requiring a strategic mind and an athletic body. Luckily, I had them both and became a part of the varsity team as a tenth grader, and I was a first-string player at that time in my high school. I started on the basketball team.

I took a keen interest in the competitions and won many accolades. The athletic phase of my life was the best; there were fewer worries and stresses—just friends and my favorite sport to play.

Basketball had my heart; it was one of the best memories I have ever made in my school. I have always been an outstanding basketball player, but my uncalled injury caused me to quit for some time. I regret it, but I could not go ahead as God had planned my fate. I wouldn't say I scored the highest ACT in school, but I wasn't that bad in my studies either. But being the best player at school gave me additional benefits, and I gradually gained popularity. Every student from the senior and junior grades started to know me well.

I was always an introvert; I had never interacted with so many people and remained in my shell until it was necessary to speak up. I think that was the reason why I never made so many friends. I barely had nights out with my boys because I had no friends to go out with me.

I indulged more in sports, where I played basketball with all the passion, dedication, and motivation I had developed within myself. It was a good thing for me. That was what I thought and believed because it helped me escape the rest of the stressful things about life. I was focused and never interested in making a huge circle of friends.

However, I still remember making friends with older guys; I was young then, and as people say, you are *influenced by your company.*

I was influenced by them, too. I wouldn't say it was for a long time that I had followed their footsteps, but yes, I did something wrong and got punished for it, too.

A Quick Departure And Return:

Another part of the several medical events on my journey will occur near or at the end of the others. At the same time, my wife and I were on our way to Arkansas for my annual cancer checkup, about a seven-and-a-half-hour drive away. While on the way, we took breaks and walked every couple of hours to prevent possible blood clots. We stopped about an hour and twenty minutes from our destiny at our daughter and son-in-law's cabin since we had promised them a visit for a while. After arriving, I lay down on the couch. Within an hour, I started experiencing a slight shortness of breath. I didn't tell anyone because I thought it would pass.

However, it was still there and even worse around four hours later. So, I decided to tell my wife. They called the paramedics, and I was checked. They found nothing but suggested I come to the hospital with them for further evaluation. However, I decided not to go with them. When midnight came, I got to where I could not breathe properly in the bed or when I sat in the large chair. They all tried for a long time to get me to agree to go to the hospital. I continually rejected the idea.

I decided that I wanted to go home. After all, I couldn't sleep because I could not breathe properly, even more so. My son-in-law said that there wouldn't be a hospital for the next three hours in the next large city going home, and if I got worse, my wife would not be able to get me anywhere medically. So, that scared me, and I agreed to go to the local hospital. I ended up being admitted and kept for nine days, getting three bags of antibiotics dripped into me per day for nine consecutive days. Come to find out, I had a severe case of pneumonia, and it almost took my life. Again, MY GOD saved my life. It taught me not to be so hard-headed anymore.

Sometimes, people came and talked to me, but I wasn't interested in making great friends. Yes, some were acquaintances, and some were mutual, but I never made any best friends because I had been in trouble once because of so-called friends. I was happy with my life; I have always believed in the "Less friend circle is better than a hundred friends." After middle school, the people I called friends, more precisely my classmates, went to different schools, and I again drifted away from them.

As I have mentioned above, I was an exceptional basketball player; I participated in tournaments in high school, and I always felt glad and special about this. I appreciated how the team needed me to win our tournaments, and gladly, we won many basketball tournaments. I can never explain my feelings accurately because it was out of this world.

Winning felt so good that I couldn't stop thinking about my winning experiences. Playing sports combined these two factors and made me feel like I was the king of basketball.

There was nothing quite like the feeling of victory; trust me when I say that. I felt great, but I was never proud. I have always been motivated to give my best. The results were on the team and my hard work.

I played in many tournaments, and we won most of them. I have received many trophies for winning basketball games, and so many people have envied me. I was an intelligent player because I always had the strategies and talent to give my best to the team and the game.

Chapter 4: Expelled

I always stood against racism because I experienced it, too. I started school at four and always made older friends who cared for me. My school life had always been great. I switched schools and finally returned to a Catholic high school.

I never had very outstanding grades; I scored more of C minus and B's, but my basketball game always saved me in more ways than one—it also saved me from getting in trouble. In addition, I represented my school in multiple tournaments.

I gained popularity with time, and people in school started gathering around me. It was an honor, but I always believed in keeping my circle small. I had a lot of experiences, and as time went on to high school, I had a lot unfold in my life.

I didn't apply myself, but I was smart. My world was surrounded by basketball. It saved me on so many occasions. Most of the guys I knew personally in school who took the ACT scored about a 13 on average, which is not a very good score. However, I appeared for the ACT and scored well; I scored 23, which was astonishing during that time and very good even now.

When the scores returned about a month later, my guidance counselor called me. He was a real racist, a big one, and I must quote the fact that he was gay, which I have learned not to judge anyone. However, he had a real problem with me for no reason, and I had noticed it for years, from when I was the age of 14 to when I was 17. I was 16 when I took the exam.

A Short Prayer: Please come to me, Lord so that I can come to you. Thank you, my Lord, for loving me so I can love myself and others. Amen.

Back to the story.

He called me, got me out of my homeroom, and I followed his footsteps. Then he took me to the side; the counselor's body language didn't seem right, but I waited till he spoke. The counselor acted as if I had burnt the school down or something; he got me and aggressively stared at me.

"Who took that test for you?" the counselor asked me.

"What test are you speaking of?" I surprisingly asked the counselor.

Fearlessly, I looked into his face and questioned what he was talking about. I had no idea until he continued with his silly questions about me.

"That ACT?" The counselor asked me interrogatively.

"I took it myself!" I told him.

"Well, how did you cheat?" he asked shockingly.

I told him I hadn't; No one could cheat taking that exam. It was a higher-level exam with so many rules and regulations. You cannot see anyone's exam paper unless you have the eyes of a falcon.

It wasn't possible, so I didn't cheat at all. But the guidance counselor didn't believe me and told me he would get to the bottom of everything. So, I had nothing to worry about because I wasn't guilty. I could have gone to any school because of my basketball and my grades on the ACT, but I managed to leave everything to fate till I tried out my luck elsewhere. In high school, there was this guy and athletic director against me. I was injured in the knee, but I learned to play independently. With my limited ability, I learned and never gave up; I was passionate about basketball, so I managed to learn everything myself. I changed my game and tried other tactics to sustain my name on the basketball team.

By that time, I had injured my other knee, too. I became angry at God and blamed Him for letting me injure my other knee when the previously injured one was not even completely healed. I was trying to adapt, and the players were now looking at me as a regular performer, while just a few days ago, I was considered a great player.

However, the blessing was that I was all on my own and learned a lot more and better than before. Now that I look back on the injuries, I realize they shaped me into a more complete basketball player. Because of the injuries, I had to go a long way in developing my basketball career, but I was still passionate about my game. I never wanted anyone to know about it. So, this one jealous football player got on my nerves so badly; he provoked me while I was on my crutches, and I was experiencing too much pain in my knee. I was so agitated by him that I lost my temper and punched him with all the force I had inside of me.

Now, that jealous guy could have beat me up, seeing me on crutches, but he was smart. He stood back, and the athletic director, the coach who always wanted me to run track, but I never would for him, came out of nowhere. The jealous guy tactfully hugged the coach and told him I had attacked him. I told the coach I hadn't played football earlier in the previous year, and he did not like that. I was passionate about basketball, but no one listened. They walked past me, and I overheard them saying, "We are going to get him out of here this time! Meaning out of the school."

I felt terrible about whatever they said but didn't take it to heart. These two guys went to the office and plotted something against me. I was unaware of the situation. I ignored it and waited for the next day to come.

The next day, my grandmother and I met with the board, and they went through my case. They made accusations about me. I understood I wrongfully raised my hand at the guy, but I had no other options. He was highly provocative in that instance.

I was disappointed to hear that the school management had expelled me; they expelled me in the middle of basketball season. But they didn't want anybody in school to know I had been expelled.

They offered me the chance to stay in school till the end of Christmas till I chose a new school. So, my doctors and a few acquaintances thought I had graduated from school. But the story wasn't framed that way; it was different because I had been expelled from my dreams and my passion because of that one jealous guy I punched in the face and the school's athletic director.

But I wouldn't say that; only the jealous guy and the athletic director were responsible for getting me in trouble. I got in trouble because of my temperament; I got angry easily. I would see that guy who got me in trouble throughout the years. We never confronted each other, but I forgave him after some time.

A Quick Departure And Return:

Whatever you take from this book, remember this: call upon it deep within your heart when you need it. You will need it at some point; it can save your life if you let it. Carrying around hate or a grudge takes so much mental energy, whether you know it or not. Whether conscious or subconscious, this hate will shape your life and bleed into the lives of those you love and who love you. You will start to wonder why those dear to you are distancing themselves. It's because of the hatred that is deep within you.

Once you experience the feeling of total forgiveness, you'll find it is a feeling that words cannot fully explain. This feeling can also change and shape your life. Whatever it takes, whether leaving a person alone or walking away from a situation, do it not just for a short period but for good. Yes, it can be challenging. But think about it. That change can and will save your life. Remember, MY GOD AND OUR GOD are watching and loving you. You must believe with all your heart and soul that it will change and save your life. Now, back to the book.

We hung out for a while and then fell out again. And different people came to me, telling me this guy was jealous. I knew he was jealous, but the best thing is people around me also felt the same as I was feeling.

People also told me that this guy was a real con man. But after a few months, I let this jealous guy go for good. I got over him, and I ultimately got him off my mind. I never had a favorite subject in school. I liked physical activities more because I wanted to play basketball and other sports. I had so many options for colleges; I could have gone to better colleges, but I ended up going to a school in Kentucky because I had an agent before time. It was illegal, but the man convinced me to sign the documents; that man's wife was a lawyer, and he knew every strategy to get me into school.

I could have gone to Loyola Marymount University and Pepperdine University. However, my agent didn't want me to fall into favoritism with the coach as the coach allowed certain players to play who were average and not on par with me. So, we decided to sign up with Kentucky State University instead.

My agent also told me that he had a good friend at Kentucky State University who would not treat me that way, and I wouldn't face any issues with him, so I trusted him. After I had signed up with Kentucky State, the coach I had initially signed up with called me to inform me that his lifelong dream to live and coach in Denver had come true. He had moved to Denver and welcomed me to accompany him, but I would have to set out for a season. I choose to attend Kentucky State.

He also told me that the coach replacing him would honor everything he promised me and that his assistant coach would be the head coach. I complied, and he sounded friendly when I talked to the new coach. I also told him my girlfriend (wife now) would join me.

He told me that I had to tell everyone that we were married because we would be living off campus, and it was decided that I would be off to Kentucky State University to attend school and play basketball. When the time came, I played well in the pre-season games and was on my way to becoming a star there. However, as time passed, the coach's attitude toward me changed. I could feel it in several ways. What bothered me the most was when he started playing this other guy more than me. This guy had been on the team for the past two years, awaiting his time, and the problematic part was that he was also the coach's recruit. And then I came out of nowhere and took his job/position, and everyone on campus knew about it.

With time, I felt like an added burden on him, and I had come out of nowhere when it was that guy's time to play. The coach had brought him in before. Considering how I joined, he had no option but to keep me.

Anyway, he played the same position but couldn't touch me. The guy wasn't on my level as I was more potent and faster, could jump higher, and, most importantly, could score the ball almost anytime.

Moreover, I did everything I could to win the coach over. I even let my girlfriend babysit his children, which was not a good idea. He was a creep, and only God and his wife stopped the coach from having his way with my girl. Later, I heard that the coach was drinking buddies with that player's father and would do everything he could to have the guy play.

When the team participated in the Chicago Basketball Tournament, word got out that my friend, the professional basketball player for the Chicago Bulls, would be coming to see me play. Hearing this, the coach didn't even let me set foot on the court during any game for no reason. He was so evil and jealous of me. I called my girlfriend, crying my soul out, and told her she would have to transfer to the University of South Alabama, my hometown. I intended to return home when the team returned to Frankfurt. When I informed the agent about what had happened, he told me to go home and start working out. He also told me he would get me a tryout with an NBA team.

So, after returning home to the city of Mobile, I got a job with the city recreation system to work out every day and prepare for the tryout.

While in California, awaiting to play in the Summer Pro League, I played in the Compton League. This league had pros like Mark Langenberger with the Lakers, Freeman Williams with the San Diego Clippers, Raymond Lewis with former Philadelphia 76ers, Michael Cooper with the Lakers at the time, and more NBA players. Even though I only played in two games, I scored 47 points the first night, and the next night, I scored 48. Soon after, I had other agents approaching me. But I had already signed up with my agent.

When I played three games for the Phoenix Suns Summer Pro League, I averaged 27.4 points a game, and I was nice enough to hook up a local guy from Mobile with a tryout. I discovered he tried to ruin my reputation, but my God stopped it. He was spreading lies to hurt me.

Chapter 5: Marriage & Children

I met my wife at the New Orleans Superdome while attending Xavier University of New Orleans. She worked part-time as an usher at the Superdome while attending The University of New Orleans. Like many other people, I had fallen in love, too. I saw her, which confirmed it for me: she was the one in that instance. She caught my eye among many, and I am forever grateful to My God to have her by my side. We were married five years later.

I grew up looking at my mother, who was very attractive and strong-willed. She was beautiful, and I always wanted someone with perfect traits like my mother. Luckily, I found my wife, who was gorgeous and my greatest support system through all of my ups and downs.

I grew up learning about norms and how life was supposed to be with the family. I adored my family; later, my wife made everything more valuable when she entered my life.

I have too much to state about my family, especially my wife. My passion for basketball was at its peak. I gained popularity because of basketball. I have learned so many different things during my life journey.

Despite being an average student, I was rather intelligent. I could learn new things because I was willing to learn; I was a keen observer. So, I made a smart move and got inspiration and help from my wife's brother-in-law. And God gave me all that I have now. I have always believed in God's plans for me; trust me, He has never failed me. My wife has always been working with me in all the businesses I have had. I sent my wife back to school; she was blessed to pursue and obtain her master's degree in Human Resources. She worked in that capacity for the city of Mobile.

I've been in businesses and excelled in all of them. It was possible because I had my wife's support throughout my journey.

I met my wife's sister's husband in New Orleans; they were well off and living luxurious lives. They never told anyone about their business but had everybody thinking my wife's brother-in-law was a pilot. They had a store that my wife's sister ran, and he was in and out of town as a pilot, but in reality, he wasn't.

Later, I discovered that he sold marijuana. He taught me how to sell large quantities of it. I was young and a keen observer, so I didn't think about the consequences of this business, but I was eager to make more money.

I was going to Florida and spoke a little Spanish since I lived in Mexico, where I played basketball. My wife's oldest brother was connected with my wife's brother-in-law. So, I told my wife's brother I wanted to go to Miami and start selling marijuana.

He took me down there, and I was in the business alone before I knew it. I even got stopped once on my way back, but fortunately, everything went smoothly. The trooper who stopped me did not even give me a ticket. I genuinely feel that MY GOD did not want me to get busted then. He pretended as if nothing had happened. My trunk wasn't opened, yet I wasn't given the ticket. In my opinion, the officer knew I was lying and ignored it completely.

I went on and on and made plenty of money like that. Nobody knew because I kept everything to myself. I made plenty of money with that business. Not many people knew about it, but I started to sell a tiny amount of cocaine, too. I got set up, busted, and was sentenced to prison for three years for trafficking in marijuana, so before I had to report to prison. I decided to drop my eventual wife back home, in New Orleans, at her mother's home and started working off-shore.

I quit that job after six months and chose to return home to my wife. I must say, my wife didn't retaliate or say a single negative word. It was three weeks on and two weeks off. I was on a semi-submersible drilling rig constructed in Japan. I was not too fond of that job. So I left after six months and came back to my family.

My wife was pregnant with our firstborn, a son. We named him Rayford the third. Everybody at the drilling headquarters wanted a job. The people at the facility took a liking to me and sent me to this Black man's office. The company had just two Black men—as tool pushers (big-time supervisors who weren't on the rigs)- in the world's largest exploration company where I worked. It was all about hard work with good money, and I was finally grateful to get into that company. It was more like a dream job for me.

I believed it was time to pay for everything my wife had gone through and done for me. We were already expecting our son and had to make decisions for our family's future.

My wife and I have four children (Rayford the 3rd, Tori, Rashad, And Morgan), and we love our children so much. My wife has always supported me. She loved me wholeheartedly and stood by my side in all problematic situations. She stood by my side and helped me when I had lost everything and all my money.

She motivated me to work hard, and whatever business I had put my hands on became a success.

A Quick Departure And Return:

We should be a miracle for other people. We should have it in our hearts to be and do something great for people.

We should put so much effort into making our lives better. As a result, we will not have time to talk or think negatively of others.

My wife is beautiful; she was stunning the moment I first met her, and she sparkles the same way even after so many years. She has been the best support I have ever had.

Yes, I got busted, caught, and lost everything. I lost whatever I had made in life. But starting over with everything was not very challenging since I had a wife every man should have. She loved me and supported me throughout.

The best thing about our relationship is that we have built a great companionship. We raised our children and taught them how a good family should live together and have each other's back in times of difficulty. These are fundamental traits that you need to prepare your children for their better future and your well-being.

Eventually, everything we did together made sense, and we lived a beautiful life together.

Chapter 6: The Sickness Kicks In

One after another, life taught me many lessons. However, nothing scared me as much as the thought of dying did. I felt shattered; I knew my days would end very soon. My heart started beating rapidly, and I was filled with sad emotions. I was worried about my family and what would happen when I, too, would be sent to God.

One day, I got very sick and ended up at the hospital. I was always running away from healthcare centers, often looking for reasons to keep myself healthy and resilient because I disliked the feeling of being at the doctor's. I had to get myself checked. I thought the checkup would be the end of it, so I went to the hospital and got myself examined.

I was diagnosed with a rare cancer known as Multiple Myeloma. This cancer is formed in the plasma of the white blood cells. Based on our body's physiology, healthy plasma cells help us fight infections by making antibodies. Whenever a foreign particle enters the body, our body releases antibodies to fight it.

However, in my condition, you will have cancerous plasma cells that accumulate in the bone marrow and deposit around the healthy blood cells. Cancerous plasma cells negatively affect normal ones, and that is precisely what happened to me.

The damage it caused was irreversible, and my body's disease-fighting mechanism was disturbed. This condition was not good news for me. It was all but confirmed; I had little to no time left. I felt awful. It seemed like it was too soon for me to be diagnosed with something like this. I told my family about my illness and braced myself for their reactions. Deep down, I knew my wife was devastated, but she motivated me to undergo treatment. With that decision, we began consulting medical experts to treat my condition.

There are multiple treatments for this cancer. My health had deteriorated due to chemotherapy—the most painful process. I heard chemotherapy was dangerous, but experiencing it was just the worst experience of my life.

I prayed to God that nobody should suffer from this type of cancer, just no one. It was painful and ruined my health rapidly. My kidneys failed later because of being on chemotherapy for three years, and my health started to feel worse. Between all this, I had lost the meaning of living life. I thought it was the end of my life, and my family would soon have to bid their goodbyes to me.

However, I still managed to keep myself strong. I pretended I was doing good to keep my loved ones happy around me. With the limited time I was alive, I thought it best to spread smiles everywhere. I didn't want to see anyone sad. I believed if I became strong, we as a family could fight anything. I prayed for my health to get better and stayed true to myself. I took medications on time and went for chemotherapies punctually.

Gradually, the fear of death made me sick, but I had to move on with life and face it all. I knew I had to keep my willpower strong and overcome negative thoughts. It wasn't easy, but I managed to help myself. I knew I could fight it, but I needed a lot of courage. My courage, motivation, and positive thinking developed with time, and I'd credit my wife for this. She has been there for me in all my difficult times. God gave me a lot of money at that time. And trust me, I only had everything I had ever dreamt of because of God. I was blessed with much property, money, and a luxurious life. But how was that going to help deal with my health?

Nothing helped; it was just the strong willpower required of me. However, when I got sick with cancer, I moved to Arkansas because the Mayor of Mobile, the first Black mayor, was diagnosed with the same kind of cancer—Multiple Myeloma, two years before me.

Multiple Myeloma is rare, but if we talk about the general statistics, then mostly Black men are diagnosed with it. My wife supported me, stayed beside me, and became my strength. Even with all my businesses, my wife stood beside me and helped me throughout my journey. She is a perfect woman, and I knew she was perfect for me the moment I met her.

Eventually, I sent my wife back to school. She had achieved her master's in Human Resources and started to work for the city of Mobile, too. I was super proud of her because she knew how to nail anything she got indulged into. She was intelligent and, most importantly, a dedicated woman.

When I got sick, my wife called the mayor for assistance. Yes, she did it for me. She was concerned about me and worried about my health. My wife immediately called me and guided me not to have my chemo therapies right away. I knew chemotherapy was a risky process. My body would change; I would lose my hair and look sick, but I had no choice other than to listen to my wife. She was consulting the best doctors for me. The mayor guided us to contact Arkansas's number-one clinic worldwide for treating Myeloma. It wasn't a simple disease. It was blood cancer, so consulting the best doctors was the only approach we had.

Arkansas had the number one doctors in the world. So, we called the hospital (UAMS). University Of Arkansas Medical Science. I asked for the doctor known for his specialty in Myeloma. I told them I wanted to see Dr. Bart Barlogie, and the receptionist told me he was very famous, and everybody wanted him, but if I could not get him, he would look at everyone's charts. They asked who referred me to that doctor, and I gave the mayor's reference.

I was blessed; I was very blessed because my reference worked at that moment. The receptionist called me back and said Dr. Barlogie would take me as his patient.

So that is how that happened; when I finally moved back to Mobile, Alabama, after the doctor had done everything he could for me, he told me that I could live for a long time as long as I took my medicine and followed the doctor's orders. But the cancer was still in my blood.

My cousin, my mother's first cousin, would come by and talk to my mother sometimes or call. But after a few years, when we met, she told me something unbelievable. It made me weep.

My cousin told me that my mother used to pray for me.

"Yeah? That doesn't surprise me because every mother should pray for their children, I responded, especially if they have cancer. I wasn't bothered much because I knew that was very common, and every mother prays for their children to get better. I was already suffering from cancer, so it was okay to know that my mother prayed for me. I was glad. However, after a few weeks, my cousin approached me again. She told me that my mother sometimes prayed and cried when my mother saw her off to the car. She worried about my health and would say, "Lord! Please take the cancer out of my son and put it in me. I don't want another child to die before me.

My brother died a few years before I came down with cancer, and his sad demise jolted our souls. We were scared, and it 3was hard for my mother to get over my beautiful brother's passing. My brother was handsome, and so was I. Finally, my mother got scared and cried and prayed for me. I knew nothing about it until my cousin told me about my mother that day.

My mother prayed to God every time, and she would always say,

"Lord, take cancer out of Ray and transfer it to."

I know that MY God heard my mother's prayers. She was diagnosed with cancer twelve years before her death, and with no signs of it ever coming back, it did when she prayed to MY GOD to take the cancer out of me and put it in her. I didn't know she was always praying for my life over hers. I was heartbroken to find out that the cancer had returned as she had asked My God to take it out of me and put it in her.

The point of stating this incident is to tell you how mothers are; they are beautiful and love their children unconditionally. I knew my mother loved me a lot, and I loved her too. I wish I could tell her how much I love her, but she was not there; she was long gone; however, after a few months of sending my blood samples to the Arkansas hospital every month. I was already residing in

Mobile, Alabama, so I couldn't travel back and forth that frequently. Anyway, after a couple of months, I got a call from the hospital, and they said, "Mr. Campbell, we looked at the sample, and it's all gone."

I didn't understand. I took my time to understand what they said, and they said it was a miracle because my cancer was gone entirely from the blood. It vanished, and we all wondered how it happened. Because the doctors told me that I could take my medicine for a long time, I took my medicine and followed the orders that the Arkansas hospital sent to the hospital in Mobile. The cancer was still in my blood, but after a few more months, it was gone entirely.

That is when my cousin told me about my mother. Probably a month after that, my mother started to become peculiar. My cancer transferred to my mother a month after that; she was admitted to the hospital and gradually took the beauty and charm away from my mother. My mom was beautiful, but she had taken all the pain for me and suffered through the pain.

God healed my sickness; one aspect was my mother's prayers and my wife's support. I had two beautiful women in my life praying for me. However, my medical journey strengthened me. I endured endless pain and a scary rollercoaster ride. I felt haunted at night, and the fear of dying was already making me numb. Out of eight patients, including myself. I'm the only one living. I will repeat it. My God did not have to save me. He did it because he wanted to. God had something else planned for me. I am still living my best life to date. Yes, I am a walking live miracle.

Chapter 7: Spiritual Journey

God has been very kind to me. I had lost all hope to live; my health was deteriorating, but I had put my faith in God and his plans. I knew he would never leave me in so much pain, and that is what happened. God changed everything for me because my mother believed in Him, and later, I became a true believer in Him.

Another incident where I remember that MY God saved my life was when my wife and I planned to attend a small evening seafood dinner at a cousin's home that I hadn't seen in years. Our wives were cooking the food, and he and I were talking until he suggested that he and I go outside and smoke a marijuana joint. I reluctantly agreed to participate even though I had not smoked in over a year, so my system was clean and pure. Even that being the case, what followed next never should have happened from just a single marijuana cigarette. To this day, I feel as though my cousin laced it with some other drug, and maybe he was trying to impress me. After smoking it, we went back into the home, and what happened next was life-changing.

I suddenly started to feel something I had never felt before. My head was getting light, and eventually, I truly felt as though something was pulling my life and spirit out of me. It was pulling from my entire body as though I was getting ready to leave my body. I heard my wife asking me what was wrong with me, but I intentionally did not answer. I needed all my strength to keep my spirit from leaving my body. They called the paramedics, and the test results said nothing was wrong with me. So, I know that My God saved my life.

I used to observe the trees around me and look closer at plants and how they grew. Nature had its way of keeping us alive and giving life to the dead. Because you can be walking and dead simultaneously, it was so amazing to see dormant seeds sprouting when they were properly taken care of.

Similarly, humans tend to stay healthy, live longer, and remain happier when given the attention, care, and love they deserve. I got immense love from my family, especially my wife, who stood by my side, and my mother, who prayed to God to transfer all the pain and cancer to her. Sometimes, I think about how mothers can be so selfless; they are beautiful in possessing unconditional love for their children. I thought about all the factors deeply and spent my days alone, investing my time thinking about life and how it was created.

A Quick Getaway And Return

Please try to take this in and absorb it. Life is beautiful and sweet. We make it hard. The decisions that we make. The people that we hang around with. And the conversations that we participate in shaping our mind and our world. Now, back to the book.

Gradually, I took time to understand what life was like and how we were supposed to make our lives better every day. Thankfully, I realized the real meaning of life is to praise MY GOD, save other lives, and do things that never disrupt the natural cycle. With that in mind, I sat back and realized that gardening was the best activity I could do.

I already knew that plants are living organisms and have a whole natural cycle, which I had studied. I started researching gardening and interviewed the residents near my house to ask about their gardening experience. Finally, I understood how the seeds were given life. The following statement is solely meant for your mind and to let the spirit take you where it wants to. Remember, in this order, JUSTIFICATION, CLARIFICATION and PURIFICATION. May My God bless you with the journey the previously mentioned words will take you on.

Miraculously, God saved my life. I knew I was going to die very soon, but the cancer was washed away from my blood. It was a miracle because nobody had ever experienced something like this before. I was alive, and I was living a healthy life. I can't explain my feelings about being alive and cancer-free. I knew God was great, and only a true believer could please God. He can make the dead alive and the alive dead.

I knew the importance of life; I realized it was necessary to live a healthy life for a longer life, so I started focusing on planting trees and a vegetable garden. I started with my surroundings because I knew real change begins with yourself. I told myself, "I should plant more trees because it was considered good work."

I got everything I needed for gardening and started doing it independently. It made me happy, and I enjoyed the garden work because I had a purpose for doing the activity; it brought me back to life.

During the days I was sick, I was in bed, all alone. I was numb, and I used to think how helpless I had become with that disease flowing freely in my blood. It annoyed me greatly, but I had no willpower to get up and try again. I was breathing but not living my life, and that is when I diverted my mind and thought about myself. Despite everything, the holy spirit guided me during my sickness. I was told to remove all of the negativity from my mind. I knew it was hard to do so, but I kept my mind positive. I managed to think about my life and felt my senses coming back.

I was numb earlier, but the thought of being positive completely changed my thinking. I became a believer and did everything guided to me by the Holy Spirit. It was a gradual progress, but I began to feel my emotions again.

I started to feel that I was alive again. It was the right time to rebuild courage within myself. I knew life was a blessing and a gift from God. We all must take our life as a gift from God and live it the right way because we never know when this gift will be taken away from us, and we will be left with nothing. So, one of the best parts about my sickness was the guidance I received.

I was told to believe again; I was motivated to feel all of the pain and fight through it. There was a voice inside my head that kept on calling me back to life. It told me never to give up because life was never a place for cowards to live. I was never a coward; I was strong. All I needed was a little push to fight all the obstacles I was experiencing during my sickness. I am so happy that I saw the light at the other end of the tunnel and grabbed my chance to stay alive again. God is great; I will always quote this.

God has blessed me with many gifts throughout my life. The precious gift was my mother. Who stayed up at night and prayed for my well-being. She possessed unconditional love for me and guided me to move on the right path in my life. Then, I had a beautiful wife who became my strength when I got sick. I never had to ask my wife for her attention. She was there for me because she genuinely cared about my health. I could see it in her eyes. Today, I am standing on my two feet, writing my story for the world to read. I'm doing it all because of my wife. She has been my strength in overcoming all the hurdles in life. Staying by my side, she never made me feel like I was losing myself or her.

The gifts and blessings from MY God held me together and reminded me I would do great things in life. I was told it wasn't the end of the world, but I had to live longer to tell everyone I was a walking live miracle!

Chapter 8: Profit & Loss

My mother told me several years earlier that I should write a book. But, I never would take the time or take it seriously. In my life, I have been blessed with beautiful things, a beautiful family, and some great experiences. Being a walking life miracle is not something many can relate to, maybe because they might have never been through certain situations.

However, I was a miracle, alive and walking around on my feet everywhere. Even though I knew I missed a significant chunk of my life during the days I was sick. But I came out stronger. I fought my obstacles because I had the best support in my life: my beautiful wife.

I believe life never goes according to your plans, and when you experience downfalls, you only come out stronger. They say it is never a good day until you experience something tragic. I have been through everything, which is why I felt grateful for getting another chance at life.

The motivation to write my story came from my lifelong experiences. I have always wanted to do something in life. Like an ordinary man who wants to support his family, I also want to support mine. And, in many ways, I did; my family was pleased with me as I was already giving them a good life.

The urge to start my own business was increasing. I gathered the expertise and experience I needed to start my work. So, I managed to launch it, but as you may have heard, a business always balances profit and loss. Yes, it was disturbing for me to solve the problems in my business, so I had to resolve them and come out of them stronger. My first business didn't work well, so I had to quit and restart everything again. Before considering other plans, I took a gap for a few months because giving myself time to rethink what I could do best was better.

Over those months, I learned about some businesses. I talked to some people regarding business ideas and understood the whole profit and loss cycle until my wife came up with the idea of launching a kid's clothing business. I knew my wife was smarter in many ways, so I got intrigued by her idea of launching our business.

The two of us invested our time in planning out the business. Together, my wife and I made a great team. We had mutual thoughts and disagreements, but working with my wife was great. She was always incredible with the design and creative side of things. I knew we were going in the right direction.

So, after everything was said and done, we launched our clothing line. It was a promising start-up initially, but maybe due to a lack of experience, we experienced significant losses that made us abandon our clothing business. From there, I started considering the uniform business for different schools.

Initially, the uniforms business was planned as a general outlet, but then I considered partnering up with different schools. My motive was never to give up and keep trying until I found something perfect to work on. I worked hard and went to different schools with a proposal in my hand. Some schools agreed to work with me, while others resisted. I found contractors to make uniforms for my business and consulted different people for more insights into the industry. I was new to it, so this business couldn't do well in the market. I met many people in my struggling days. Some people gave me honest suggestions, while others just pulled my leg. I knew I was stronger and better than any problem coming my way, so I never took anything to my heart.

I worked hard until I switched my interests and started my mortgage firm. I knew I was making a tough decision, but I had made my decision and started working on it.

My wife was a great support; she supported me after initiating the business. MY God blessed me to start the business. Once I learned about it. I acquired $2,250,000 worth of real estate with $753,000 worth of equity personally, my actual income not for the business. Which was done in 14 months. I was very confident about flourishing in this sector until I started experiencing the real estate crunch in 2008 through the 2010 market crash. So, I could not flip the properties, and my customers could not get financed. I could not refinance to get any equity out of the properties, and I had terrible luck lingering on me.

After that, I was diagnosed with cancer and had to move to Arkansas to the best Multiple Myeloma cancer center in the world. I experienced a bad loss in my business and had no property management helping me out. So I couldn't stand up again. It felt like a significant part of me was taken away, and coping with the loss had become difficult for me. It was heartbreaking for me because I lost 10 of my 17 properties. I tried to be strong, but nothing helped until my wife came, sat with me, and told me, "Profit and loss are a part of the business. Falling multiple times won't weaken you; it will make you stronger."

My wife's words made me feel stronger, and I came out of the losses I had experienced in my businesses.

One of the other experiences that shaped me and opened my eyes was our children's elementary school and the local school board that the school was within. It was a magnet school, and our children were accepted initially. However, discovering what was happening there would take about four years.

Things started because one of our children's teachers sat me down one day while I was picking up the children. What she told me hit the core of my spirit. She informed me that what she would say didn't include our children. However, it included several other small Black kids at the school. The first thing she said was that some of the White teachers were letting the Black kids drink out of certain water fountains and White kids drink out of others. The next thing was that some of the White teachers were intentionally teaching some Black kids to fail. One of the reasons was that when the Black kids could not keep up with the standards, they would have to transfer to a regular school.

Then, when that happens, the Black children are replaced with White children who could not get into the school from the beginning because of the government's ratio. However, the ratio doesn't apply when replacing the Black kids during the school year. So, the teacher asked if I would attend an already-arranged meeting after school. I went to the meeting, and the initial thing that began my life-changing experience was that I accepted the position of being the face of making it all public and bringing it all to light. What was said, "You, Mr. Campbell, are in business, and they cannot hurt you. We work for many of these people, and they can upset our lives."

I thought about it, and what came to my mind was that if I or my family needed help from being in such a situation, I would want someone to help me, not knowing that it would send my wife and me into total bankruptcy and change our lives. Our family never had a problem with the school before we started to ask questions about what was happening there.

Well, once I saw that there might be some validity to some of the things mentioned in the meeting, I decided to recruit others to help my wife and me. I thought this would be easy, but it was far from that. The first person I tried to get to join was my cousin, who didn't have kids there anymore and who was ten years older than I was at the time, and he had lots of experiences in life. After telling him what was happening, he advised me to drop it all and take care of my family. I asked him why he would tell me such a thing.

He responded, "The White people that are doing these horrible things are vicious with lots of venom in their hearts, and he will not be able to help me. I responded, "It's almost the year 2000. Come on and help me and the kids out," but he didn't.

However, it only made me more determined, even if I had much to lose. I kept thinking, what if my family and I needed help? Where do we get it from? Eventually, we got about eight people out of over 20 who we had asked. I could not believe it; we were helping people afraid to help their kids. Well, the word got out that my wife and I were trying to help and expose what was happening at the school; they put the word out that we were the face of the campaign. We started to get phone calls along with meetings from Black individuals who worked for and within the school system, acting as if they were going to bond with us and bring it down. However, they were all seeking information to betray us and our cause.

One of the individuals warned me because he felt we were good people, so he said, "Those teachers would ostracize you and your children from the school. Hence, I want you to know what you are getting into and what's ahead of you and your wife." I will indeed be as honest as I can. I had to reconsider what was said because the school treated our children well. Well, my wife followed my decision, and we went forward.

Things began to change right away. Almost all of the teachers distanced themselves from me and my wife. So, we made sure that we asked our children about everything that happened that day at the end of every school day. Thank God they were in the first, second, and fifth grades and could communicate well. For the most part, they didn't bother our kids so badly. However, they came after me and my wife with a vengeance. As I reflect on this part of our lives, I am getting some of the same feelings I felt back then, and they are almost as strong. I must break as often as possible so the thoughts won't ruin this Sunday.

One of the first things that happened was that one of our businesses, "Campbell's School Uniforms, a cinch to win the nomination from our area for National Minority Small Business Of The Year, was suddenly removed from the list for no reason. When my doctor friend's wife was asked to come to one of the school board members' offices, I considered her at sale-out first. This means people who would give their souls for money and a position in this life, even if it hurts kids or innocent people. When his wife met with the person who was on the school board, he tried to convince her that my wife and I were some hateful people. Little did he know the doctor's son was one of the children being mistreated. The school board representative asked her to tell us, the Campbells, that we could lose our livelihood and to distance her and her husband from us. The doctor told me he was and is still a general doctor, which means he doesn't depend on referrals as specialists do, so those people could not affect his practice. The doctor's wife asked the school board member what he meant by that statement concerning the Campbells losing their livelihood.

He said that the schools could order $50,000 worth of a certain uniform and then change their minds on the order. They did follow through on that threat. Another major act the school board superintendent was behind was Campbell's uniforms, along with the only other school uniform store in the city serving public schools at that time. The superintendent instructed the school principals to pass out only the other school uniform store flyers to the parents and not to pass out Campbell's uniform flyers. The previous school year, our uniform company only made $100,000 gross; it was our second year, and we took the risk and went into that business, hoping that school uniforms would become mandatory in Mobile County very soon.

Well, it just so happened the following year. So, when you look at the math, there were 66,000 public school kids, and by the uniforms being a start-up the first year, each child would spend from $300 to $500, and the ones that qualified for it received an $800 voucher from the state social program. So, our company was supposed to make several million dollars between the two stores. We only did about $60,000. We couldn't understand what happened until a little old white lady entered the store to purchase a uniform belt for her grandson. What she told us was hard to believe. She said the school only passed out one flyer, directing her to the other uniform company. She thought we had gone out of business from the previous year or did not carry her school's uniforms.

After she informed us of what had happened at her school, we started to investigate. We found that every school principal had been advised to do the same thing. We were heartbroken and eventually had to shut down the uniform company. We survived off of our mortgage company for as long as we could. However, the inevitable came to pass, and we lost almost everything. The debt was too overwhelming, so the hatred cost us our livelihood. Oh, but let me say it was tough for a few years, but MY God gave it all, and even more, back to us as he did to Job in the Bible, and we keep going and growing in our faith and the wisdom that our God was giving us.

Chapter 9: Incarcerated

You make and learn from mistakes; it all adds to your experiences. Indeed, like many, I've made mistakes. I believe we all do at times. However, the key is to learn from these missteps. Such experiences contribute to understanding ourselves better and foster a positive outlook on life.

From the onset of my life's journey, I've experienced countless heart-wrenching moments. I recall instances where, despite my best efforts to safeguard them, things slipped through my fingers, leaving me with far less than what I'd started with. I struggled to remain steadfast for as long as possible, but the weight of sorrow persistently cast a shadow over me.

I started out being in the minimum security section of the prison. However, when my grandmother and wife used to visit me, I would have coin money left over after the visits. I didn't know that the money was considered contraband. Eventually, after one of the visits, one of the guards was told that I possessed money.

The guard confronted me, and it led to a physical fight. Because of this, I was sent to maximum security lockup, a different environment. It was everything one might imagine it would be and more. Upon arriving there, I was placed in solitary confinement and lost all of the good times I had accumulated, which meant that I would have to serve my entire sentence, three years. That was another instance where God intervened, and in his own time, I earned all of the good time back and completed my sentence on time. However, that transfer and those experiences were never to be forgotten. A person has to be truly blessed and guarded by the most divine power to have gone through a penitentiary sentence and to come out undamaged because of the brainwashing, temptation, sorrow, and pain. All of the things you are exposed to within the system blend back typically into society and rise very high in every business I have pursued.

I take no credit for it; it was and always has been MY GOD, the highest that did it all. So, I say to you, don't you ever give up. It is only the enemy trying to distract you. You must focus on the Lord God at those times, and it will go away. Remember, this is a lifestyle; trusting in MY GOD is not just a one-time thing. However, it will get easier as you do it more and more; it will be your new lifestyle, and you must believe in it with great faith and confidence.

One of my other experiences in which MY GOD had protected me from getting into even deeper trouble was that on one of my trips back from Miami, I was stopped by a Florida State Trooper while carrying a hundred pounds of marijuana. In my heart, I feel that with all of his experience, he had to have known that I was holding something illegal. God had to have come over him. He was so pleasant and let me go. Also, at the time, I had a case for trafficking in Marijuana back in my home state of Alabama pending.

My hard-earned properties ran out of my hands like sand seeping through my fist. These properties were not obtained with illegal money. I was losing my properties one after another, and I started experiencing so many losses in my life's journey. I was at my breaking point, but I knew I had to keep calm and see what would happen next. My personal life was great; my wife was supportive and motivated me to find myself again because it was a part of life. Some days, you gain the best you expected; others, you lose everything. Life is never static; it continues to challenge you in its ways, and I have been challenged a thousand times.

It was always my wife who supported me when I first started to run a business and even during the most challenging times when I was suffering from cancer. I was a walking live miracle and had developed a unique mindset. I knew there would be a good phase in my life again, where I would be reminiscing the hard times.

The mistakes I talked about at the start of this chapter were a hint to my story when I was incarcerated. I made a mistake without knowing its consequences, and I regret it.

Incarceration is a big thing in your life; if you have ever been in prison, you are stamped with the curse that comes along with it for a lifetime. Life is not normal; you are away from your family and must adjust to the new jailed environment until the period ends. The life of a prisoner is very different from that of the outside world. Speaking your heart out or giving suggestions is not allowed, and that leaves a lasting impression on your mind and your soul.

Landing in the prison was nothing but a nightmare for me. It was a completely new life I would experience, and I didn't know for how long. When I knew the end of my sentence was only a few days away, I decided to tell the guards that my life was being threatened. It was known that when a person was either ending a sentence or going out on probation, there was a great possibility one or more inmates would try to get the inmate that was left in trouble. The perfect example is the evening when I was packed and going for the trailer that was considered my safe house. An inmate that I knew well asked me to deliver a marijuana joint to another inmate along the way. I told him no, and he smiled and said, "You don't want to get in trouble, do you?"

With everything within me, I knew I was being set up for trouble and not going home to my family. I would have caught another case within the system and spent more time in prison. This is another example of how our God protects and guides us. All we have to do is pay attention and obey.

Well, I was incarcerated for trafficking marijuana, and my brother-in-law was the person who initially helped me to get into the business when I asked him to help me do so. He informed me about this guy who was going to Miami to purchase a significant amount of marijuana. I got intrigued and asked him to connect me with his link and buy me some.

I knew my brother-in-law hadn't visited Miami in many years, and going there with him was a new experience. So it was around two in the morning when we arrived in Miami, and we had to drive until daybreak to locate the connection's house; things were not very direct in this marijuana business. To purchase the weed, we had to go through a series of groups and then finally met the dealer. However, we tried to search for the connection's house, and it turned out the house belonged to his mother.

I stayed in the vehicle, and my brother-in-law was in the front yard dealing with the connection. I don't know what they talked about, but my brother-in-law told the connection that we were here for business and needed the stuff. Meanwhile, the connection was called by his mother, and later, he called to tell us there was no deal happening. My brother-in-law knew this was a big city, and whatever we needed was easy to find, so it was better to search elsewhere instead of trying to convince someone who wasn't interested in the business we were giving them.

We kept on searching, and the first set of people that we asked were two gay guys. We asked them if they knew where we could purchase a quantity of marijuana, and they consented to linking us with someone. However, in return, they asked,

"How do we know that you guys are not the police?"

They were right in their stance, so to prove that we were not the police, we went to this hotel and rented a room. My brother-in-law shot cocaine into his arm to prove that we were not police.

Then they asked my brother-in-law,

"Well, what about him?" they asked about me, but I firmly believed that I would not do what he was doing. So, we all proceeded to this super high-rise building, and there we were introduced to a Haitian man who then took us to a Cuban guy who spoke decent English. I was a great basketball player in Aguascalientes, Mexico, and spoke decent Spanish. We were glad to finally meet him because we were a step closer to what we wanted to achieve. This was our first connection.

By then, I knew whom to contact if I ever needed marijuana. So I went there again on my own. Starting from the bottom, I purchased eleven pounds of marijuana. And just for kicks, I also bought two ounces of cocaine, which were not for me to sell, and I didn't want to get into that arena either. But I was so lured by it that I bought them. After I had it all in my hand, I called my little and only brother to let him know everything went well and I would be returning the next day.

Here is the part I regret the most. I shouldn't have told my brother about it because later, I discovered that my little brother had told one guy back in the old neighborhood, which was almost like telling the police themselves. My brother did not mean anything by it. But he did it.

After several more trips, I was bringing back large amounts of marijuana each time. On one trip, I got my girlfriend with me, who is currently my wife and always has been with me. I want my readers to note that I was young and did not realize how dangerous this was.

I had multiple visits to Miami, where I had bought and consumed drugs on a large scale. There was this one time when the Cuban guy brought a neighborhood fortune teller or someone of that pursuit into his home, and without my permission, she began to pour rubbing alcohol onto the floor. I concentrated on something else until I saw fire. She then started walking in a fire with her bare feet and chanted some unfamiliar Spanish words, which gave me a weird feeling.

I recall her repeating, "Dice, Dice," multiple times while spitting fire out of her mouth. I questioned the Cuban man about why she kept reiterating those words. He said she said that the spirit was speaking to her. And then comes the most interesting part: she said, "I'm going to be a millionaire in real estate."

The lady had no idea who I was. I must admit, after 14 years, I had completely lost all of it without using any illicit funds. In just 14 months, I obtained real estate valued at over $2,253,000 by opening a mortgage firm.

Soon after all of this happened, I was so hooked up on drugs that I completely lost myself; I frequently started consuming them. I was freebasing it. I started snorting it at first and later smoking it. There were only three individuals who were aware that I was basing cocaine secretly. My sleep cycle was disturbed, and I wouldn't sleep for stretches of three days straight. On one occasion, after an insomniac bout, my grandmother had left a message, which I had left unheard. So, after I woke up, I checked my voicemail recorder, in which my grandmother said, "Boy, you better wake up. With those burglar bars covering every window and door, you will roast alive inside the house in the event of a fire."

I also had a best friend who gave me good advice, and the best advice that he could give me was to leave drugs forever and never look back on it because these things had severe consequences to bear. He further told me to stop before it was too late and that he didn't want to see me through trouble just like he did. I did not listen, leading me to let my guard down and get busted.

I ended up receiving a three-year mandatory sentence for trafficking in marijuana. My wife had just gotten pregnant, and we had recently purchased a home. So, my wife had to start working many extra hours at the hospital. Before going to the larger state prison, I was put in the local county jail until I could be processed and transferred to the state facility. While I was in the local prison, the Catholic priest came to see me. However, there was nothing he could do for me besides pray for me. I arrived at the state processing facility and stayed there for about a month, waiting to be transferred to the permanent prison. It was arranged for me to be in a minimum-security prison at that time. During the entire process, I thought about all my wrong choices. I knew I had made a mistake that caused these consequences and had to live with it.

I wasn't aware of the life of prisoners; it was my very first experience. I hadn't even read anything about their lives, and when I was jailed, I learned new things every day.

An older inmate told me that before the new guys came in, other inmates asked to find out who knew who. It was evident that I would not let anyone take advantage of me. When I started playing basketball, and the word got out about how good I was, almost everybody gravitated toward me. They saw my skills and decided to speak to me openly.

The head sergeant there offered me a job because of my education. I turned it down and took a job in the dorm because I wanted more access to the outside. After a couple of months, I tried transferring jobs and got assigned to the kitchen.

Everything was fine for a while. Then, I had a severe encounter with an inmate who had been watching me for a while. We had words, and before I knew it, he pulled out the largest butcher's knife I had ever seen. However, it was only MY GOD who saved me and kept him from using that knife. I don't know, but for some reason, he disliked me, and I couldn't take it. I stood up to him even though I did not have a weapon. I wanted to fight him or ask him about his real problem with me. My face-off with that guy was breaking news, and news rolled out that I didn't get intimidated by him. I did not know it, but he was known for using a knife on other inmates in the past. That is why he had such a long sentence in prison, and he had nothing to lose by cutting or stabbing me. So, the sergeant transferred me out of the kitchen to another job. This was another incident where MY GOD saved my life.

After the horrible incident in the kitchen, I stayed a lot more to myself. I did not even play basketball anymore. I mainly concentrated on my family and got closer to God because I knew God was always there for me.

One morning, we were in line for breakfast when I noticed an inmate looking sickly. I asked him if he was doing okay. His name was Carlos. He just looked at me while he was slowly going down and hanging onto the burglar bar prison cell door. Carlos was always sick, and I knew he wasn't feeling good then. He did not answer me when I asked him if he was ok. He did not answer for a second time. So, I asked him if he was dying because even he knew his time was near.

I remember everyone in the line was staring and assessing the situation. They couldn't stand up for Carlos or extend their hands to help him because they feared the consequences. In these situations, you are supposed to call the guards first, and they would take action, but I did not feel there was enough time to wait for someone to come. So, I picked him up and ran with him in my arms to the prison infirmary hospital. One of the prison guards was running behind me, screaming behind my back and asking me to stop, but I never stopped until I reached the hospital.

AT THIS TIME LET US PRAISE MY GOD AND YOUR GOD.

PRAISE THE LORD, I TELL MYSELF, WITH MY WHOLE HEART, I WILL PRAISE HIS HOLY NAME. PRAISE THE LORD, I TELL MYSELF, AND NEVER FORGET THE GOOD THINGS HE DOES FOR ME. HE FORGIVES ALL OF MY SINS AND HEALS ALL OF MY DISEASES. HE RANSOMED ME FROM DEATH AND FILLED MY LIFE WITH LOVE AND TENDER MERCY. AND MY YOUTH IS RESTORED LIKE THE EAGLES.

AMEN.

I knew I would get scolded for doing this, but I had no other option. A man was dying right in front of my eyes, and I couldn't see it happening without my trying to help him. I got scolded, but because of the severity of the situation, I was not punished. Sadly, Carlos died, and it was all over the prison that I ran with Carlos in my arms, with the prison guards scolding me after that. I became a hero in the prison and got appreciation from everyone.

Eventually, after my sentence period was over, I received a phone call from a lawyer, and he asked me if I would testify as to what had happened concerning Carlos. I replied yes because I wanted to testify for Carlos and his family. However, his mother received some wrong information about me. She called me next and used some curse words for me. I calmly talked to her because she thought I was scared that the authorities might revoke my probation, but I told her that was not the case. I had served my sentence, and I was not afraid of anyone. If I had been fearful, I would never risk my well-being trying to save his life. And I did not appreciate any of what she was saying. I assured her that I would testify only because of Carlos, not because of the nasty things she was saying to me. She never apologized to me, and she hung up the telephone. The family received a settlement, and I have never heard back from her again.

After I was released, I was happy at how MY God saved me from all the danger in the prison, and I survived. I was thrilled because I would now be with my wife and baby boy. I was mentally, spiritually, and physically free from all the negativities. The darkness that was surrounding me started to fade away.

Finally, I was back in my life once again...!

Chapter 10: Faith and Belief

In the final chapter of my journey, which shows every step of my life, from the innocence of early childhood to the great depths of faith and belief in the later years, we have been reflecting on an extra special life. From the kind memories of a divorced family to the diligent challenges and triumphs of education, each chapter has seamlessly discussed various aspects of life filled with resilience and determination. The early decision to join the basketball team shaped my high school experience, along with accolades and recognition, and set the stage for confronting and overcoming adversity. Whether it was the unfair dismissal from school due to racial discrimination or the joy and support found in marriage and raising children, each experience has contributed to a rich picture of life.

My diagnosis of blood cancer, kidney transplant, and a pacemaker implant were massive turning points in my life, bringing to light the fragility of health and the indomitable spirit required to face the darkest moments. But the support of my loving wife and the guidance of the Holy Spirit became hope in my hopeless life as the journey took a more introspective turn toward spirituality and understanding God's presence in every trial. From the excitement of launching a clothing line to the humility of experiencing loss, business ventures taught valuable lessons in perseverance and faith.

Perhaps one of the most challenging chapters of my life was incarceration, where I experienced the power of divine protection and the firm strength of faith. Each chapter, with its struggles and successes, has been a stepping stone to a deeper understanding of life's purpose and the transformative power of faith. Remember, practice it, then preach it. Today, when I am surrounded by family, enjoying the simple pleasures of gardening, and reflecting on a life that could only be described as miraculous evidence of the power of faith, the journey has come to an end. Today, my health condition is proof of divine intervention and belief's healing power.

Throughout the journey of this extraordinary life, faith has been the golden thread I have held for a long time. It was ever-present and evolving, guiding me at each step through the various challenges. From the earliest days of childhood through the trials of health, incarceration, and the rollercoaster of entrepreneurship, faith has been not just a companion but my center of strength and existence. It has been a light in the darkest times, offering hope when circumstances seemed unbearable and peace amid the storms of life.

My life has been filled with moments where faith was tested to its limits. Sometimes, the shadows of doubt and despair blur the path forward. Especially my diagnosis of cancer, the heartbreak of business failures, and the worst part of being held in prison were not just challenges to overcome but were the hardest lessons to learn. Though fraught with hardship, these encounters acted as crucibles within which a deeper, more resilient faith was forged. My true essence of belief was challenged, yet it emerged stronger, purified by trials, and reaffirmed through each victory, no matter how small. This faith was an active acceptance, a spirited force that threw forward movement, even when the end could not be seen. It was the strength to stand still against the strongest waves of an ocean, the courage to accept God's will, and the wisdom to see divine grace in every result. The belief system, built stone by stone through each experience, has become a personal worship and a legacy to pass on. A proof of faith's power to transform, heal, and transcend the trials of the human experience.

The never-ending journey of faith reminds me that belief is not a destination but a continuous path of growth, learning, and understanding. It is a journey that does not promise ease at any step but offers the assurance that we are never alone and that all things are possible with faith.

My journey is shaped by faith in MY God. This faith has been a source of strength during tough times and has profoundly influenced my outlook on health, life, and the difficulties that come my way. Now, when I recall my hard times, it's clear that my belief system has been the guiding light through the storms, offering solace when there were no answers and imbuing me with a sense of purpose that transcends the mundane.

My strong faith has taught me to consider health a holistic harmony between mind, spirit, and body. My battle with cancer was horrifying, but it became a recoverable path with the power of faith. During the long nights in the hospital, amid the stress and fear, I truly grasped the meaning of surrendering to a higher power. Because I was helpless, this surrender gave me profound strength and helped me. It also showed me that some battles are fought on a different plane, where faith is the most potent weapon. Doubt was an inevitable companion on this journey; it has often cast its blurry shadows on my faith, challenging its foundations and tempting me to despair. There were moments when I used to doubt the essence of a benevolent creator due to some minor inconvenience in life. These moments of doubt were intense periods of questioning and seeking, a natural response to the incomprehensibility of life's hardships. Overcoming these doubts did not happen overnight, nor through a single epiphany, but it took time. It was a gradual and often painful process of fighting with my beliefs, seeking understanding in the Scripture, and experiencing the tangible manifestations of God's presence in my life.

In sharing these personal reflections, I aim to convey that faith, with all its complexities and challenges, is a profoundly human experience. It is an excellent gift from God in this journey that invites us to embrace our vulnerabilities, seek meaning beyond our struggles, and find a source of enduring hope and strength in God. This journey is as much about the moments of doubt as it is about the moments of pure belief, for it is through these experiences that our faith becomes truly our own and shows the transformative power of a relationship with the divine.

As we close this book on the narrative of hope, resilience, and the power of faith, I wish to leave you with a final reflection and a heartfelt call to faith and belief. The essence of this journey, encapsulated in the title "A Walking Live Miracle," is proof of miracles through my personal story, and it is also an invitation to recognize the miracles that faith can unfold in each of your lives.

Humans worldwide experience different kinds of challenges and trials since they are inevitable. Yet, it is crucial to remember that giving up on oneself or losing faith in God is a choice we should promise ourselves never to make. In the moments when surrendering seems to be the easiest way out, we must hold onto our faith in God and His miracles with the greatest tenacity.

Believe in the Divine, the goodness within and around us, and the path itself. This firm faith can transform the hardest situations into the easiest ones, turn despair into hope, and manifest miracles in our everyday lives.

A Quick Departure And Return:

The devil/Satan is looked upon and referred to as a dragon. We must be dragon slayers.

I urge you to let my life be a source of inspiration, a thread of hope whenever you doubt your faith, and a reminder that you can overcome impossible situations, navigate through the storms, and emerge stronger on the other side. I have chosen "*A Walking Live Miracle*" since it declares the power of faith, a narrative of surviving against the odds, and a message of hope for everyone who reads it. This journey of faith has shown that miracles are not just ancient tales or rare encounters but are real and active in our daily lives. I'm a miracle for other people, and I want to be.

A Quick Departure And Return:

Before I share the last miracle, I must tell you about this experience to remind you that MY GOD is always in control. My wife and I left on a Wednesday for my six-month cancer check-up in Arkansas. The previous Saturday, I had a clear tube removed from my right carotid artery, which had been intentionally left there for about a year. Initially, out of embarrassment, I would have it removed each time I went home, but the repeated removals and reinsertions caused significant scar tissue to develop in my carotid arteries. This made reinsertion difficult, so when I had kidney surgery, a vascular surgeon implanted the tube to avoid future issues.

It stayed in place for almost a year but was never needed. About a week before our trip to Arkansas, I noticed the back of my hand swelling badly, which then spread up my arm to my elbow and eventually to just below my neck, near the carotid artery. I called the doctor, thinking the swelling would subside, but he scheduled surgery to remove the tube, discovering it had caused a blood clot. However, fragments of the clot had scattered through my body and lodged in my lungs, unbeknownst to me at the time.

On our way to Arkansas, we visited our daughter and her husband at their cabin. After lying down for only two or three hours, I felt strange but kept it to myself, hoping it would pass. When it didn't, I finally told my wife, who, along with the others, convinced me to call an ambulance. The paramedics couldn't find anything wrong but recommended I go to the hospital, which I declined. Later that night, I couldn't lie on my back without immense pain and struggled to breathe. I insisted on going home, but my son-in-law advised that the nearest hospital was three hours away in Jackson, Mississippi, and if my condition worsened, I'd be in serious trouble. Reluctantly, I agreed to go to the hospital.

Upon arrival and examination, the doctors diagnosed me with severe pneumonia. They were concerned about the infection spreading to my pacemaker, as infections gravitate rapidly to foreign objects in the body. They wanted to proceed immediately to check if the infection had reached my pacemaker, but I preferred to go home for the procedure. The doctor agreed only if I remained under a doctor's care. The situation was still serious despite receiving three bags of antibiotics through an IV every 24 hours. After nine days and 27 bags of antibiotics, I decided to have the procedure. The results showed the infection had not reached my pacemaker. I thank MY GOD for saving my life again. This is another example of His power, wisdom, and love. Remember, MY GOD DID NOT HAVE TO SAVE MY LIFE; He did it because He wanted to. My grandmother used to say when something was factual and serious: NOW, PUT THAT IN YOUR PIPE AND SMOKE IT.

By the way, just to let you know, on my last visit to the multiple myeloma clinic, I was made aware that the clinic has a new test that can go into a myeloma cell to the millionth degree and see if either of two categories exist. The way I understood it is that the first category tells that the cancer will never come back, which MY GOD put me in. The second category tells that if the cancer should come back, I will be a ninety-year-old man or even older at that time. So, I'm cancer-free. MY GOD, YOUR GOD, OUR GOD has healed me.

This book/message is about the miracle(s) in my life and your life if you believe and talk to the most high, the one and only, MY GOD. We can only get to him through Jesus Christ—who lived and died for us all.

REMEMBER, REFER TO GOD AS MY GOD. You should take possession of him because he is your God. You must claim him as being such. The enemy cannot influence you during these times.

These miracles manifest through restored spirits, healed bodies, and transformed lives. Each step toward faith in God is a miracle in movement, a promise to the unseen hands to guide, provide, and protect us. Let us all be living miracles, embodiments of faith in action, and evidence of what belief can truly achieve.

I LEAVE YOU WITH THIS SPECIAL AND POWERFUL PRAYER THANKING MY GOD AND YOUR GOD FOR ALL OF THE TIMES HE HAS SAVED OUR LIVES.

I love the Lord because He hears and answers my prayers, and because He (bends down and listens), I will pray as long as I have breath. Death had its hands around my throat, and the terrors of the grave overtook me. I saw pain and sorrow in that deep, dark hole—the grave. But then, I called on the name of the Lord.

I said, *"Lord! Please save me."* What a good God MY GOD is, So kind, so merciful this God of ours is. The Lord protects those of child-like faith. I was facing death, and then he saved me. Now I can rest again; he has been so good to me. He saved me from death, my eyes from tears, (many, many, many) tears, and my feet from stumbling. And so, I walk in the Lord's presence as I live here on Earth.

Amen.

www.ingramcontent.com/pod-product-compliance
Lightning Source LLC
Chambersburg PA
CBHW072038150726
47999CB00002B/972